Mood Food

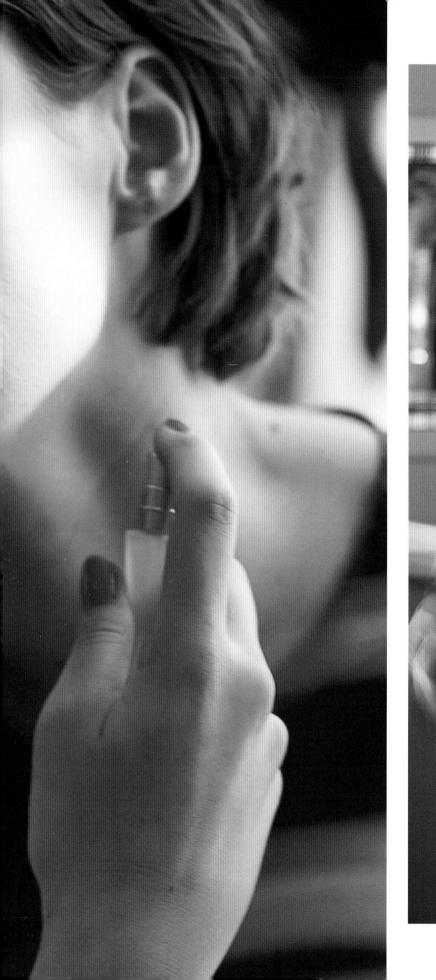

Mood Food

hamlyn

First published in 2000 by Hamlyn
an imprint of Octopus Publishing Group Limited
2–4 Heron Quays, London E14 4JP

Distributed in the United States by
Sterling Publishing Co., Inc.
387 Park Avenue South, New York NY 10016-8810

ISBN 0 600 60186 2

Printed in China

Creative Director	Keith Martin
Executive Art Editor	Leigh Jones
Senior Designer	David Godfrey
Production Controller	Lisa Moore
Editor	Sarah Ford
Assistant Editor	Sharon Ashman
Picture Researcher	Rosie Garai
Special Photography	Paul White
Model	Kirsten Symonds
Stylist	Akoiko

Acknowledgments

Decadent chapter shot on location at
Carolyn Corben's flat. Romantic chapter
shot on location at The Savoy Hotel,
The Strand, London WC2R OEU.
Wild chapter shot on location at
Shari and Bill Maryon's house, Bristol.

Picture Acknowledgments

Arena Images/ Hanyachlala 107
Image Bank/ Antonio Rosario 67
The Interior Archive/ Simon Brown 130
Octopus Publishing Group Ltd. /Jean Cazals 13,
28,133 /Gus Filgate 124 /Colin Gott 91,122 /Sandra
Lane 2 right, 4-5, 7, 12, 18-19, 19, 40, 41, 42, 45,
49, 52, 58, 62, 68, 79, 81, 82 Top, 90, 95, 102, 105,
121, 127, 131, 135 /Gary Latham 34-35, 46 /David
Loftus 3, 11, 17, 24, 47, 64, 66, 86, 92, 93, 97, 101,
104, 106, 109, 112, 123 /James Merrell 27, 100
/Neil Mersh 32, 33, 57, 59, 114, 140, 141 /Hilary
Moore 51, 110 /Peter Myers 103 /Sean Myers 31,
37, 56, 71, 99, 119 /Peter Pugh-Cook 36 /William
Reavell 1, 6, 16, 23, 50, 53, 73, 84, 87, 94, 96, 111,
113, 115, 118, 125 /Salvatore 60, 75, 88-89, 134,
138 /Simon Smith 132 /Ian Wallace 21, 48, 63, 65,
68-69, 70, 72, 76, 78, 80, 82-83 /Philip Webb Front
Cover, 15, 38, 44, 55, 74, 77, 85, 129, 137, 139
Tony Stone Images/ Bob Krist 108

Notes

- Eggs should be medium unless otherwise stated.
- Milk should be whole unless otherwise stated.
- Pepper should be freshly ground unless otherwise stated.
- Fresh herbs should be used unless otherwise stated. If unavailable, use dried herbs as an alternative but halve the given quantities.
- Ovens should be preheated to the specified temperature. If using a fan assisted oven, follow the manufacturer's instructions for adjusting the time and temperature.

Contents

Introduction

A mood is simply a state of mind. Our moods affect everything we do and the way we do it, and particularly what we feel like doing. You might, for example, feel in a particularly wild state of mind, tempted by the idea of taking on new challenges and attempting something that you've never had the nerve to try before. Or you might be totally at ease with the world and feel like putting your feet up, spending a quiet time and allowing nothing to intrude on your relaxed mood. Or you may feel eager for a decadent, self-indulgent bout of pampering in the way that you are sure you deserve. Or perhaps you are in an active, energetic, get-up-and-go frame of mind, with a wish list for an hour in the gym, a brisk walk in the park, and getting to grips with all those pressing jobs that you've been meaning to finish for weeks. Or you may even be in the mood for love, with dreams of romance and quiet evenings alone together.

Go with the flow

Our moods are influenced by a whole host of factors. These include the time of year, the weather, and the foods we've been eating, but, more importantly, the people around us. An argument, for example, can change your mood, or a smile from someone in the street. Even the mail you receive can change the way you are feeling. However you feel, it's always important to let yourself to be led by your mood. Allow yourself be guided by the way you feel because if you try to do something at odds with your mood, you're unlikely to do it well. A little of what you fancy does you good, so wear what you like, do what you want, and cook whatever you desire.

Changing moods

Moods can change unexpectedly. Just because you were in an active frame of mind yesterday, doesn't mean that you'll feel the same today. Perhaps now a new day has dawned, you favor a relaxed mood, with nothing on the agenda other than sitting and reflecting.

Your mood is perhaps the most influential thing in your life. It can affect everything you do and the way in which you do it. This also applies to the food you want to eat and the way you want to cook. We've taken five moods—decadent, active, relaxed, wild, and romantic—and suggested dishes you will feel like cooking when you are in those moods.

A decadent mood

Everyone needs to be pampered from time to time, and food is one of the most effective ways of doing this. So if you're feeling deliciously decadent, go on and spoil yourself. You will find dishes in this chapter that are laced in luxury and extravagance to delight your taste buds and give you a lift.

Try Rich Polenta Salad, for example, which succeeds in putting the wickedness back into salad, or for a real treat, make Peppered Tuna Steaks with Fennel, Red Onions and Sugar Snap Peas, and delight in a colorful medley of flavors. Chicken with Cream Cheese, Garlic, and Herbs elevates this ubiquitous meat to something rich, luxurious, and utterly delicious. Chocoholics are bound to agree that Hot Chocolate Crêpes were invented in heaven. And, as if that isn't enough, there is also a wildly extravagant Champagne cocktail with vodka, peach schnapps, and peach juice, which is pure self-indulgence.

An active mood

Full of beans and raring to go? Now's the time to dash into the kitchen and create something wonderful. When you're feeling active, you'll want to stun your senses with crunchy textures, dazzling colors and startling flavors to maintain that energy high. None of the recipes in this section take long to prepare and before you know it, you'll find yourself cooking up a sensational spread of delectable dishes.

There's nothing quite like grilling to get you on your feet, or like lemon to activate all the senses, so try Grilled Tiger Shrimp with Mint and Lemon and you'll be ready for anything. Or perhaps you'd rather surprise your taste buds with Spicy Beef Koftas in Pizzaiola Sauce, in which chile and garlic share pride of place. When you use up lots of energy, then you need refreshing long drinks. Limeade and Grapefruit Mint Cooler taste great and put you back on top of the world.

A relaxed mood

Cooking is fun but slaving over a hot stove is quite definitely not. For those days when you are feeling laid back and relaxed, you want to cook something that is easy and, preferably, quite speedy. Quick doesn't have to be boring—far from it—and the clever cook will be able to concoct something utterly delicious, high on flavor but low on labor, which you will then be able to savor in a hammock in the garden, or in front of your favorite film.

Try Toasted Radicchio and Fontina Bruschetta with Anchovy Relish, for example, which will take you just fifteen minutes and yet get your taste buds buzzing with pleasure. Or rustle up a quick pasta dish of Fettucine with Smoked Salmon and Asparagus Sauce, which takes less than half an hour to prepare. Risotto is always tasty, but many people dismiss it as being too complicated and time-consuming to prepare. Just allow yourself to be taken over by the repetitive stirring process, and you'll be surprised at how much more relaxed you feel when you dig into the delicious result than when you started. And to take the final curtain, Bananas in Coconut Milk take just minutes to prepare for a truly scrumptious dessert. So unwind, relax, and enjoy yourself!

A wild mood

There will be days when you're in the mood for being wild and want an adventure, when you feel like a challenge and you've got more than the usual time and energy to spare. Trying out an entirely new, untested recipe can present you with a welcome challenge.

Try Steamboat Soup from Cambodia, for example, and serve an out-of-the-ordinary, cook-at-the-table hotpot of poached seafood in an aromatic stock of startlingly tart ingredients, garnished with cilantro and sweet basil leaves and slices of chile. Or take a trip to Tunisia and serve deep-fried phyllo turnovers, called briks, or try your hand at Lamb Tagine with Okra and Almonds, flavored

with a subtle mixture of garlic, ginger, spices, and honey. Thailand has a lot of ideas to offer the wild cook, and Crisp Fried Fish with Chile and Basil is sure to please the most discerning eater. Finally, go to India for dessert, with delicious ice creams flavored with pistachio and saffron, and decorated with edible gold or silver leaves.

A romantic mood

Certain foods are well known for their passionate persuasions, such as shrimp and oysters, asparagus, chiles, and chocolate, and when you are feeling romantic, nothing else will do. The recipes in this chapter are sensuous and tantalizing for those evenings for two, whether it is a candle-lit supper or a cozy night on the couch. All are quick to prepare to allow you more time with your loved one, and less time in the kitchen alone.

Conjure up a Mexican Soup with Avocado Salsa, for example, a fiery dish to arouse the passions, which reflects the rich colors and contrasting moods of Latin America, cooled by the subtle smoothness of avocado salsa. Oysters are well known for their aphrodisiac qualities, so we suggest you try Deviled Oysters and see if they live up to their reputation. If you're having a quiet evening in, we suggest you cuddle up on the couch together and share a plate of scrumptious Crispy Wrapped Shrimp. Lobster has always had sexy connotations, so try Grilled Lobster Tails with Oregano Butter for a special occasion—with luck, you'll agree it was worth the expense. And for dessert, we suggest Passion Cake, which is so-called for a very good reason. Wash it down with Blue Champagne, the ultimate in romantic drinks.

Decadent

Appetizers and snacks

Main courses

Desserts

Drinks

If your mood is one of utter decadence, this chapter is for you. It's sure to provide you with all the ideas that you need to indulge yourself shamelessly. You will find dishes here to pamper your taste buds, and a choice of luxurious, wicked foods to linger over and luxuriate in, with the creamiest sauces, the richest cheeses and—needless to say—the smoothest, most sensuous chocolate flavors. And as if that weren't enough, there are also some extravagant cocktail recipes with which to give yourself the occasional lift. So give yourself up to the delights of these tempting recipes and spoil yourself.

Rich polenta salad

These bars of polenta and goat cheese—rich and creamy, thick and buttery—are just the thing to add a touch of luxury and excitement to your salads.

2½ cups water

1 cup quick-cooking polenta flour

2 tablespoons butter

8 oz goat cheese, rinded

1 small radicchio head, separated into leaves

4 oz arugula

3 tablespoons extra-virgin olive oil

1 tablespoon balsamic vinegar

salt and pepper

1 Heat the water to a gentle simmer, pour in the polenta flour and beat well for 1–2 minutes until it is a smooth paste. Turn the heat down and continue to cook the polenta until it thickens, stirring constantly so that it does not catch on the bottom of the saucepan or form a skin on the top; it needs to cook in this way for 6–8 minutes.

2 When the polenta is thick and cooked, add the butter and season with salt and pepper; mix well. Pour it on to a chopping board and spread to ¾ inch thick and allow to set for 5 minutes.

3 Thinly slice or crumble the goat cheese and spread it on the polenta, then cut the polenta into bars or wedges. Place the polenta under a preheated hot broiler and cook until the cheese has melted and started to bubble.

4 Put the radicchio leaves and the arugula into a bowl. Add the oil and vinegar, and season with salt and pepper, then toss the leaves until coated. Arrange the salad leaves on individual plates and place the polenta bars on top.

Baked reblochon

A crisp puff-pastry case, bursting with rich, bubbling cheese, will make one of life's magical moments.

8 oz puff pastry, thawed if frozen
1 small Reblochon cheese
1 egg yolk mixed with 1 tablespoon water
sweet chutney, to serve

Oven temperature: 425°F

1 Divide the pastry in half and roll each half out on a lightly floured surface to form a thin square.

2 Take the cheese and, using a very sharp knife, cut away the rind. Sit the Reblochon in the middle of one pastry square, brush around the cheese with a little egg yolk mixture, and then top with the second pastry square. Press all around the edges to seal well and then trim the pastry to give a 1-inch border.

3 Transfer the pastry to a baking sheet and leave to chill for 30 minutes. Brush the top and sides with more of the egg yolk mixture and score the top with a sharp knife to form a criss-cross pattern. Cut 2 small slits in the top of the pastry to allow the steam to escape.

4 Preheat the oven to 425°F. Bake the pastry for 20 minutes until it is puffed up and golden. Allow to stand for about 10 minutes, then cut into wedges and serve with chutney.

Spicy zucchini fritters

Serve these spicy zucchini fritters as a special treat, topped with smoked salmon and sour cream.

1 lb zucchini, grated

1 egg, beaten

2 tablespoons all-purpose flour

1 chile, seeded and chopped

1 garlic clove, crushed

¾ cup shredded Cheddar cheese

salt and pepper

dill sprigs, to garnish

To serve:

6 oz smoked salmon

⅔ cup sour cream

1 Heat a griddle or nonstick skillet. Squeeze the excess moisture out of the grated zucchini—the best way to do this is to place the zucchini into a clean dish towel and squeeze well.

2 Mix the egg and flour until smooth. Add the zucchini, chile, garlic, and cheese. Mix well and season to taste with salt and pepper.

3 Place spoonfuls of the mixture on the hot griddle or in the hot skillet, flatten with a palette knife, and cook the fritters for 4–5 minutes, then turn and cook for a further 4–5 minutes. Do not disturb them while they are cooking, as a crust needs to form on the cooking side, otherwise they will be difficult to turn.

4 Keep the cooked fritters warm and repeat until all the mixture has been used. Serve the fritters between layers of smoked salmon and sour cream, and garnish with sprigs of dill.

Variation: Spicy Potato Fritters

Replace the zucchini with 1 lb peeled and grated potatoes. Squeeze the moisture out of the potatoes and make the fritters following the main recipe.

Sichuan scallops

This recipe hails from the region of Sichuan in western China. Hot and fiery, it is intended for the boldest palates.

2 tablespoons oil

1½ lb scallops

2 garlic cloves, crushed

1 dried red chile, finely chopped

½ teaspoon Chinese five-spice powder

1-inch piece of fresh ginger, peeled and finely shredded

2 tablespoons Chinese rice wine or dry sherry

2 tablespoons dark soy sauce

3 tablespoons water

6 scallions, diagonally sliced

1 small onion, sliced

1 teaspoon superfine sugar

2 scallions, shredded, to garnish

1 Heat the oil in a wok or heavy-based skillet until smoking hot. Add the scallops and sear on both sides, then remove and reserve.

2 Add the garlic, chile, five-spice powder, and ginger and stir-fry for 1 minute. Add the wine or sherry, soy sauce, water, scallions, onion, and superfine sugar, and stir-fry for 1 minute more, then return the scallops to the wok and stir-fry them in the sauce for no longer than 2 minutes or they will become tough.

3 Arrange the scallops with their sauce on a warmed serving dish and garnish with the scallions.

Peppered tuna steaks with fennel, red onions, and sugar snap peas

1 First prepare the vegetables. Remove the feathery fronds from the fennel bulbs, chop finely, and reserve. Trim the root ends of the fennel and discard. Cut the fennel in half lengthwise, then cut into ¼-inch thick slices. Cut the onions into rings. Top and tail the sugar snap peas or snow peas and cut in half lengthwise on the diagonal. Peel the potatoes.

2 Heat the oil and butter in a large skillet. Fry the fennel slices gently for 5 minutes, then add the onions. Cook over a moderate heat until the fennel and onions are tender, then increase the heat to color slightly. Remove from the heat and keep warm. Boil the potatoes until tender.

3 Meanwhile, coarsely crush the peppercorns with a pestle or the end of a rolling pin. Mix with the salt. Brush the tuna steaks with the olive oil and press in the pepper mixture to coat. Heat a large skillet over a moderate heat. Set the steaks in the dry skillet and fry for 2 minutes on one side, then turn and fry for 1 minute on the second side.

4 Add the sugar snap peas or snow peas to the fennel and onion mixture with the fennel fronds and toss over a high heat until hot. Drain the potatoes, cut each one into 4–5 slices, and keep warm. Transfer the tuna to a warmed dish and keep warm.

5 Turn the heat up under the skillet. Add any remaining cracked pepper, pour on the brandy and a little of the stock, and stir to scrape up the sediment and any fish juices. Let the mixture bubble fiercely for a few seconds, then add the rest of the stock and the lemon juice, and boil rapidly until syrupy.

6 Remove the skillet from the heat and gradually add the butter pieces, stirring to combine them with the sauce and thicken it. Add the cream, still stirring to mix well. Bring to a boil and boil for a few seconds, then add the chopped parsley and reduce the heat. Keep warm while serving the fish.

7 Divide the vegetables between 4 warmed plates, arranging them in a mound in the center. Set a tuna steak on this and pour a little of the peppered sauce on top of each steak and around the edge of the vegetables. Garnish with parsley sprigs and serve immediately.

Tuna is a firm, meaty fish, well deserving of this exciting treatment with an interesting medley of garden vegetables.

19

¼ **cup black peppercorns**
1 **teaspoon salt**
4 **x 5 oz tuna steaks**
1 **tablespoon olive oil**
¼ **cup brandy**
⅔ **cup concentrated fish or chicken stock**
3 **tablespoons lemon juice**
¼ **cup sweet butter, cut into small dice**
⅔ **cup heavy cream**
2 **tablespoons finely chopped parsley**
4 **flat-leaf parsley sprigs, to garnish**

Vegetables:
2 **fennel bulbs**
2 **red onions**
1 **cup sugar snap peas or snow peas**
4 **potatoes**
2 **tablespoons olive oil**
2 **tablespoons sweet butter**

Fish in wine sauce

Make this delicately flavored dish with lemon sole, or try sea bass fillets if you want a more robust texture.

12 oz white fish fillets, skinned

1 egg white

2 garlic cloves, finely chopped

1 tablespoon cornstarch

1⅓ cups peanut oil

salt and pepper

1 tablespoon chopped cilantro, to garnish

a few drops of chile oil, to serve

Wine sauce:

1 cup hot chicken stock

6 tablespoons Chinese rice wine or dry sherry

1 tablespoon cornstarch

½ teaspoon sugar

2 tablespoons chopped cilantro

1 Cut the fish into bite-sized pieces. Put the egg white and garlic into a bowl with salt and pepper to taste and whisk with a fork until frothy. Sift in the cornstarch and whisk to mix. Add the fish and stir until coated.

2 Heat the oil in a wok until very hot but not smoking. Deep-fry the fish in batches for about 2 minutes each until crisp and lightly golden. Lift out with a slotted spoon and drain on paper towels. Very carefully pour off all the hot oil from the wok and wipe the wok clean with paper towels.

3 Next make the sauce. Pour the stock and rice wine or sherry into the wok and bring to a boil over a high heat. Blend the cornstarch to a paste with a little cold water, then pour it into the wok and stir to mix. Simmer, stirring, for 2 minutes until thickened.

4 Add the sugar and stir to dissolve, then stir in the chopped cilantro. Return the fish to the wok. Stir the fish very gently to coat it in the sauce and heat through for 1–2 minutes, then taste for seasoning and add more sugar, if liked. Serve very hot with a few drops of chile oil and garnished with cilantro.

Chicken with cream cheese, garlic, and herbs

Chicken breasts are tender and special any time, but this herb, garlic and cream cheese stuffing nestling between the skin and flesh, makes them ultra-special.

4 boneless chicken breasts

½ cup cream cheese or low-fat soft cheese

3 tablespoons finely chopped mixed herbs (such as tarragon, dill, parsley, chervil)

1–2 garlic cloves, crushed

1 tablespoon butter

salt and pepper

green salad, to serve

To garnish:

lemon wedges

rosemary sprigs

Oven temperature: 425°F

1 Insert your fingers between the skin and the flesh of each chicken breast to make a pocket.

2 Put the cheese in a bowl with the herbs, garlic, and salt and pepper to taste. Beat well to mix. Push the cheese mixture into the pockets in the chicken breasts, dividing it equally between them. Smooth the skin over the cheese to make it as compact as possible.

3 Melt the butter in a small saucepan, then use to brush a baking dish. Arrange the chicken breasts in a single layer in the dish, then brush with the remaining butter and season with salt and pepper to taste.

4 Preheat the oven to 425°F. Bake the chicken for 20 minutes or until it is cooked through and tender when pierced with a skewer or fork.

5 Serve the chicken hot, cut diagonally into slices if liked, garnished with lemon and rosemary sprigs. A green salad would make a good accompaniment.

Stuffed baked lamb

This is a magnificent Moroccan dish—just the thing for those occasions when you want to entertain a crowd in style.

4 lb boneless leg of lamb

1 onion, cut into thick wedges

3 tablespoons olive oil

½ cup lemon juice

green beans, to serve

Stuffing:

½ cup couscous

⅔ cup boiling water

2 teaspoons coriander seeds

2 teaspoons cumin seeds

1 teaspoon ground cinnamon

3 tablespoons olive oil

¼ cup pine nuts

½ cup slivered almonds

1 large onion, finely chopped

2 garlic cloves, crushed

1 teaspoon dried mint

¼ cup chopped cilantro

⅓ cup raisins

salt and pepper

Oven temperature: 475°F

1 First make the stuffing. Put the couscous into a bowl, pour over the boiling water, stir, then leave until the water has been absorbed.

2 Heat a small heavy-based saucepan, add the coriander and cumin seeds, and heat until fragrant. Grind to a powder, then mix with the cinnamon.

3 Heat 1 tablespoon of the oil in a skillet, add the pine nuts and almonds, and fry until browned. Transfer to paper towels to drain. Add the remaining oil to the skillet. When it is hot, add the onion and fry until soft. Stir in the garlic and spice mixture and fry for 2 minutes, then add the couscous, nuts, mint, cilantro, raisins, and salt and pepper to taste.

4 Open out the lamb, skin side down, on a work surface. Season inside with pepper, then spread over the stuffing. If possible, tuck the flaps of the piece of lamb over the stuffing. Roll up the lamb into a neat sausage shape, then tie securely with string.

5 Preheat the oven to 475°F. Put the onion wedges into a roasting pan that the lamb will just fit. Put the lamb on the onion and pour over the oil and lemon juice. Bake for 15 minutes. Lower the oven temperature to 425°F, and bake for a further 25 minutes so the lamb is still pink in the center. Remove the lamb from the oven, cover, and leave to stand in a warm place for about 15 minutes before carving. Serve with green beans.

Venison cutlets with red juniper pears

Pears in red wine, usually a dessert, are also excellent served with rich venison cutlets to make a memorable meal.

4 firm dessert pears

2 tablespoons lemon juice

1¼ cups red wine

6 juniper berries, crushed

pared zest of 1 lemon, cut into julienne strips

1 cinnamon stick

3 tablespoons red currant jelly

8 venison cutlets

oil or melted butter

watercress sprigs, to serve

1 Peel the pears, then halve them lengthwise and remove each core with a melon baller. Brush the flesh with the lemon juice to prevent the pears from discoloring.

2 Combine the wine, juniper berries, lemon zest and cinnamon stick in a saucepan. Bring to a boil, add the pears, cover, and simmer gently for 10 minutes or until tender.

3 Transfer the pears to a bowl with a slotted spoon and set aside. Stir the red currant jelly into the liquid remaining in the pot and boil until reduced by half. Pour over the pears and leave to cool.

4 Brush the venison with a little oil or butter. Cook under a hot broiler or on a barbecue for 2–3 minutes on each side. To serve, place 2 cutlets on each plate and add a portion of pears. Serve with sprigs of watercress.

Zuccotto

This is a luxury dessert *par excellence*. The traditional decoration for zuccotto is alternate stripes of confectioner's sugar and cocoa powder sifted over the top.

3 large eggs

6 tablespoons superfine sugar

½ cup all-purpose flour

1 tablespoon cocoa powder, plus extra for dusting

1 tablespoon oil

Filling:

¼ cup brandy

1½ cups heavy cream

4½ tablespoons confectioner's sugar, sifted

2 oz bittersweet chocolate, chopped

¼ cup almonds, chopped and toasted

1 cup cherries, pitted

2 tablespoons Kirsch

Oven temperature: 350°F

1   Place the eggs and superfine sugar in a heatproof bowl and whisk over a saucepan of hot water until thick. Sift the flour and cocoa powder into the bowl and fold into the egg mixture, then fold in the oil.

2   Preheat the oven to 325°F. Spoon the dough into a greased 8-inch cake pan and bake for 35–40 minutes. Turn on to a wire rack to cool.

3   When cool, cut the spongecake in half horizontally and line a 2-quart bowl with one layer. Sprinkle with brandy. Whip the cream to soft peaks. Fold in 3 tablespoons of the confectioner's sugar, the chocolate, almonds, cherries, and Kirsch. Spoon into the bowl and top with the remaining spongecake. Cover with a plate and chill.

4   Turn out on to a serving plate, then sprinkle with the remaining confectioner's sugar and cocoa powder to make a pattern.

Hot chocolate crêpes

As any chocoholic would agree, there is nothing more luxurious than these pancakes, sinking in a hot chocolate sauce.

Crêpes:

¾ cup + 2 tablespoons all-purpose flour

2 tablespoons cocoa powder

2 tablespoons superfine sugar

1 egg

1¼ cups milk

oil, for frying

Filling:

1 piece preserved ginger

2 tablespoons superfine sugar

1 cup ricotta cheese

⅓ cup raisins

5 oz white chocolate, finely chopped

3 tablespoons heavy cream

Chocolate sauce:

½ cup superfine sugar

½ cup cold water

6 oz bittersweet chocolate, broken into pieces

2 tablespoons sweet butter

2 tablespoons brandy (optional)

Oven temperature: 400°F

1 First make the crêpes. Sift the flour and cocoa powder into a mixing bowl. Stir in the sugar. Add the egg and a little milk, and whisk to make a stiff batter. Beat in the remaining milk.

2 Heat a little oil in a medium skillet, then pour off the excess. When the skillet is very hot, pour in a little batter and tilt the skillet so the batter coats the base. Cook over a moderate heat until browned on the underside.

3 Flip over the crêpe with a palette knife and cook the other side. Slide the crêpe out of the skillet and keep warm while you make 7 more crêpes.

4 To make the filling, finely chop the ginger and mix in a bowl with the sugar, ricotta, raisins, chocolate, and cream. Place a spoonful of the filling in the center of each crêpe. Fold into quarters, enclosing the filling.

5 Preheat the oven to 400°F. Arrange the crêpes in a shallow ovenproof dish, then bake for 10 minutes until heated through.

6 Meanwhile, make the chocolate sauce. Heat the sugar and water in a small heavy-based saucepan until the sugar has dissolved. Bring to a boil and boil for 1 minute. Remove from the heat and stir in the chocolate and butter. Stir until dissolved, then add the brandy, if using. Serve with the crêpes.

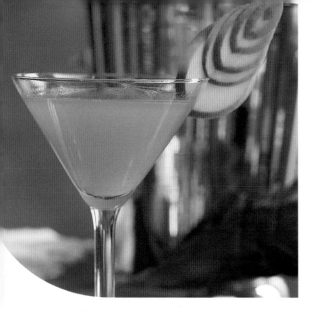

Bellini-tini

Preparation time 2 minutes Serves 1

This slightly effervescent mixture of vodka, peach schnapps, peach juice, and Champagne is the ultimate in self-indulgence.

2 measures vodka
½ measure peach schnapps
1 teaspoon peach juice
Champagne, to top up
peach slices, to decorate

1 Pour the vodka, peach schnapps, and peach juice into a cocktail shaker. Shake thoroughly. Pour into a cocktail glass and top up with Champagne. Decorate with the peach slices.

Sapphire martini

The piercing blue of Curaçao speaks volumes about luxury. Add a cocktail cherry and you couldn't ask for more.

ice cubes
2 measures gin
½ measure blue Curaçao
1 red or blue cocktail cherry (optional)

1 Put the ice cubes into a cocktail shaker. Pour in the gin and blue Curaçao. Shake well to mix. Strain into a cocktail glass and carefully drop in a cocktail cherry, if using.

active

You're bursting with energy and raring to go, so now's the time to whip up a storm in the kitchen. None of these dishes will take long to prepare and they will get you singing and dancing your way around the kitchen at the drop of a whisk. You won't sit still for a minute because there's no rest for the wicked and you'll be quite literally chopping, slicing, dicing, stirring, blending, griddling, firing up your wok, and lighting those coals. Bright colors, contrasting textures, and dazzling flavors will all shock your taste buds into action and keep you feeling full of beans, fighting fit, and overflowing with energy.

Yellow bell pepper and tomato pizza

The contrasting textures and colors of the brightest yellow peppers and red cherry tomatoes are sure to put a spring into your step.

2 large ripe tomatoes, sliced

12 red cherry tomatoes, halved

1 cup seeded and sliced yellow bell peppers

4 sun-dried tomatoes in oil, drained and sliced (optional)

2 teaspoons grated lemon zest

12 black olives, pitted

olive oil, for oiling and drizzling

salt and pepper

basil leaves, to garnish

Pizza dough:

2 cups strong all-purpose flour, plus extra for kneading

½ teaspoon salt

½ teaspoon active dry yeast

½ cup warm water

1 tablespoon olive oil

Oven temperature: 450°F

1 To make the dough, sift the flour and salt into a large bowl and stir in the yeast. Make a well in the center and gradually stir in the water and oil to form a soft dough. Turn out onto a lightly floured surface and knead for 8–10 minutes until smooth and elastic. Place in an oiled bowl. Turn the dough once to coat the surface with oil, then cover with oiled plastic wrap. Leave to rise in a warm place for 45 minutes, or until doubled in size.

2 Knead the dough lightly and divide into 2 equal pieces. Roll out each piece of dough to a 9-inch round and transfer to 2 oiled pizza plates or a large oiled baking sheet.

3 Arrange the tomatoes, yellow pepper, sun-dried tomatoes, if using, lemon zest, and olives over the dough. Season well with salt and pepper, and drizzle with a little olive oil.

4 Preheat the oven to 450°F. Bake the pizzas at the top of the oven for 20 minutes or until the bases are crisp and the top golden. Garnish with the basil leaves and serve hot or cold.

active

There's nothing that will keep your spirits up quite like a dish full of freshness and vitality. Grilling is fun, so get to it ...

Grilled eggplants

4 eggplants, sliced into rounds, or baby
  eggplants, sliced lengthwise
1 large bunch of basil
⅔ cup pine nuts, toasted
1 garlic clove
¾ cup grated Parmesan cheese
grated zest of 2 lemons
¼ cup lemon juice
3 tablespoons olive oil
salt and pepper

1   Heat a grill pan or nonstick skillet until hot. Place the eggplant slices on the hot surface and cook for 3 minutes on each side, then remove and arrange on a serving dish. Repeat until all the eggplant slices are cooked.

2   To make the lemon pesto, place the basil, pine nuts, garlic, Parmesan, lemon zest and juice, and olive oil in a food processor or blender, season with salt and pepper, and process until smooth.

3   Drizzle the lemon pesto over the eggplants and serve with crusty bread.

Variation: Grilled Zucchini with Lemon Pesto

Use zucchini instead of eggplants, cut them lengthwise into thick ribbons, and cook as in the main recipe. Serve drizzled with lemon pesto.

with lemon pesto active

Vegetable beignets

1½ lb assorted vegetables, such as bell peppers, zucchini,
    baby corn, eggplant, onions, French beans, cauliflower,
    and mushrooms
sunflower oil, for frying
herb sprigs or salad leaves, to garnish
garlic mayonnaise or sweet and sour sauce, to serve

Tempura batter:

1 large egg
1 cup beer, very well chilled
1 cup all-purpose flour
½ teaspoon baking powder
salt and pepper

Oven temperature: 375°F

Serve this medley of fresh vegetables in crisp, puffy Japanese tempura batter with garlic mayonnaise or with sweet and sour sauce. Your taste buds will be working overtime.

1 Cut the peppers lengthwise into ¼-inch thick strips. Cut the zucchini into flat batons about ⅛ inch thick and the eggplants into slices on the diagonal about ⅛ inch thick. Cut the baby corn in half lengthwise, the onions into thin rings, and the French beans into 1½-inch lengths. Cut the cauliflower into florets and parboil them for 2 minutes. Drain and refresh. Leave the mushrooms whole if small, or cut in half if large.

2 About 20 minutes before cooking, prepare the batter. With a small wire whisk, beat the egg in a large bowl. Still beating, add the beer in a thin stream. Sift the flour, baking powder, and a pinch of salt into another bowl, stir in pepper to taste, and tip on top of the egg and beer. Stir with the whisk, barely enough to mix; don't overbeat. Cover and leave to stand for about 10 minutes.

3 Heat the oil to 375°F, or until a cube of bread browns in 30 seconds. Dip the vegetables in the batter, one type at a time. Fry no more than 6 pieces at once or the temperature of the oil will drop and make the batter greasy. Zucchini, onions, cauliflower, baby corn, and mushrooms take 3–5 minutes; peppers, eggplants, and beans about 3 minutes. The batter should be puffy, crisp, and golden, the vegetables just tender.

4 Preheat the oven to 375°F. Transfer the vegetables to an ovenproof dish or tray lined with paper towels and keep warm in the oven until they are all cooked. They will stay crisp for about 30 minutes.

5 Arrange the beignets on a large platter around a bowl of sauce, or pile about 9 beignets in the center of each plate and put a few spoonfuls of sauce on the side. Garnish with herbs or salad leaves and serve immediately.

Grilled tiger shrimp with mint and lemon

There's nothing quite like grilling to get you dancing in the kitchen, or like lemon to activate the senses!

1½ lb raw tiger shrimp, peeled and deveined, heads removed

1 large bunch of mint, chopped

2 garlic cloves, crushed

½ cup lemon juice

sea salt and pepper

mint leaves, to garnish

1 Place the shrimp in a glass mixing bowl. Add the mint, garlic, and lemon juice, season to taste. Allow to marinate for 30 minutes or overnight.

2 Heat a grill pan or nonstick skillet until hot. Place the shrimp and marinade in the pan and cook for 2–3 minutes on each side. Serve garnished with mint leaves.

Spicy baked fish

A firm, meaty fish stuffed with a tangy mixture of herbs and bread crumbs and topped with garlic and chile—an assault on the senses, but a welcome one.

3–4 lb sea bass or porgy, cleaned, scaled, and filleted
juice of 2 limes
6 tablespoons olive oil
deep-fried onion rings, to garnish

Stuffing:
2 cups fresh bread crumbs
¼ cup butter, melted
1 tablespoon finely chopped chives
1 teaspoon finely chopped cilantro
1 small green bell pepper, cored, seeded and finely chopped
½ onion, grated
grated zest and juice of 1 lime
pinch of grated nutmeg
salt and pepper

Topping:
2 tablespoons oil
1 small onion, chopped
1 garlic clove, crushed
1 red chile, seeded and chopped
1 tablespoon chopped cilantro
¼ cup fish stock

Oven temperature: 350°F

1 To make the stuffing, put the bread crumbs into a bowl and mix in the melted butter, then all the remaining ingredients. Blend well, cover, and set aside.

2 Wash and dry the fish fillets and place in a large dish. Sprinkle with the lime juice and season inside and out with salt and pepper. Set aside in a cool place for about 1 hour to marinate.

3 To make the topping, heat the oil in a skillet and add the onion and garlic. Fry gently until the onion is softened and golden. Add the chile and continue cooking for 2–3 minutes, then stir in the chopped cilantro and fish stock.

4 Preheat the oven to 350°F. Remove the fish fillets from the marinade and sandwich together with the stuffing. Fasten with skewers or wooden toothpicks. Pour over the oil and any remaining marinade, and scatter the topping mixture over the fish. Bake for 20 minutes, then serve garnished with deep-fried onion rings.

active

Laksa

An authentic Asian dish that is a meal in itself; a tantalizing coconut and chicken broth is poured over fresh noodles and finished with chopped scallions, red chile, and roasted peanuts.

3 tablespoons peanut oil

2 large onions, finely chopped

4 garlic cloves, crushed

3 red bird chiles, finely chopped

¾ cup chopped roasted peanuts

1 tablespoon ground coriander

1 tablespoon ground cumin

2 teaspoons turmeric

5¼ cups coconut milk

1 teaspoon shrimp paste (optional)

1–2 tablespoons sugar, to taste

2 cups shredded cooked chicken

2 cups beansprouts

1 lb fresh flat rice noodles

4 scallions, chopped

3 tablespoons chopped cilantro

salt and pepper

To serve:

4 scallions, chopped

1 large red chile, finely sliced

1–2 tablespoons chopped roasted peanuts

1 Heat the oil and fry the onions until golden brown. Add the garlic, chiles, peanuts, ground coriander, cumin, and turmeric, and fry for 2–3 minutes or until the spices have cooked through and released a strong aroma.

2 Stir the coconut milk and shrimp paste, if using, into the spice mixture, cover the pot and leave to simmer for 15 minutes. Season the spiced coconut with salt, pepper, and sugar to taste. Add the shredded chicken and half of the beansprouts to the coconut mixture and simmer for 5 minutes.

3 Blanch the fresh noodles in boiling water and divide between 4 large warmed bowls. Sprinkle with the scallions and chopped cilantro, and divide the remaining raw beansprouts between the bowls.

4 Ladle the chicken and coconut mixture over the noodles and serve with chopped scallions, sliced red chile, and roasted peanuts.

Stir-fried duck

In this modern recipe the sweet, juicy fruitiness of mango counteracts the richness of duck meat and tempers the fieriness of red hot chile.

with mango

1 large boneless, duck breast (magret), weighing about
   13 oz, or 2 small duck breasts
1 ripe mango
¼ cup peanut oil
1 large red chile, sliced into very thin rings
¼ cup Chinese rice wine or dry sherry
3 oz Chinese mustard greens (gai choy), torn or shredded

Marinade:
2 tablespoons light or dark soy sauce
1 tablespoon rice wine vinegar or white wine or cider vinegar
½ teaspoon chile oil
1-inch piece fresh ginger, peeled and grated
½ teaspoon Chinese five-spice powder

1 Strip the skin and fat off the duck and discard. Cut
the duck flesh into thin strips, working diagonally
across the grain, then place them in a non-metallic
dish. Mix together the marinade ingredients, pour
them into the dish, and stir to mix. Cover and leave
to marinate at room temperature for about
30 minutes.

2 Meanwhile, cut the mango lengthwise into three
pieces, avoiding the long central stone. Peel the
pieces of mango and cut the flesh into strips about
the same size as the duck strips.

3 Heat a wok until hot. Add half of the oil and heat
until it is hot. Add half the duck and stir-fry over a
high heat for 4–5 minutes or until just tender.
Remove the duck with a slotted spoon and repeat
with the remaining oil and duck.

4 Return all of the duck to the wok and sprinkle with
the chile and rice wine or sherry. Toss to mix, then
add the mango and mustard greens, and toss for
1–2 minutes, just until the greens start to wilt.
Serve immediately.

active

Get marinating, get squeezing, and get flaming with these delicious pork kebabs, accompanied by a tart grapefruit salsa.

Pork and juniper kebabs with ruby grapefruit salsa

1 lb boneless pork, trimmed and cut into
   1½-inch cubes
about 16 bay leaves

Marinade:

1 ruby grapefruit

2 tablespoons lime juice

3 tablespoons clear honey

2 garlic cloves, crushed

6 juniper berries, finely crushed

½ cup walnut or olive oil

Salsa:

2 ruby grapefruit

2 tablespoons chopped chives

2 tablespoons very finely chopped red onion

salt and pepper

1 To make the marinade, squeeze the juice from the grapefruit, working over a bowl so that no juice is wasted. Stir the remaining marinade ingredients into the bowl of juice and mix well. Add the pork cubes, turn to coat thoroughly, then cover and leave to marinate for 1–2 hours.

2 To make the grapefruit salsa, chop the grapefruit segments and place them in a bowl. Stir in the chives and onion, season with salt and pepper, then set aside.

3 Remove the meat from the marinade and thread onto 4 skewers, placing a bay leaf between each piece of meat.

4 Place the kebabs under a preheated moderate broiler or on a barbecue and cook for 15–20 minutes, turning and basting frequently with the remaining marinade. Serve with the grapefruit salsa.

Spicy beef koftas in pizzaiola sauce

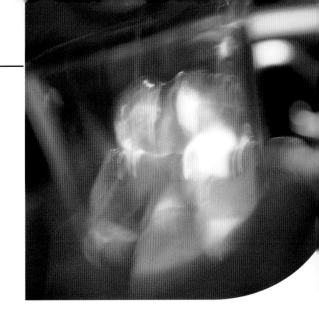

Leap into action with these meatballs in a spicy sauce, in which fresh chile and garlic play a starring role.

1 egg
1 cup coarse fresh bread crumbs
1 lb lean ground beef
6 tablespoons grated onion
2 tablespoons all-purpose flour
2 tablespoons sunflower or olive oil
salt and pepper
flat-leaf parsley sprigs, to garnish

Pizzaiola Sauce:
1–2 tablespoons sunflower or olive oil
1 large onion, finely chopped
2 garlic cloves, crushed
1 red chile, seeded and finely chopped
1–2 red bell peppers, cored, seeded, and
    chopped
1½ cups canned plum tomatoes
1¼ cups beef stock
2 tablespoons tomato paste
2 tablespoons finely chopped basil
1 teaspoon finely chopped oregano
1 tablespoon chopped flat-leaf parsley
pinch of sugar
½ cup black Kalamata olives, pitted

1 First make the koftas. Beat the egg in a large bowl, stir in the bread crumbs and add the beef and onion. Season with salt and pepper. Work together until well combined. You will find that your hands are best for this. Divide the mixture into 8 portions, shape each one into a ball and roll in a little flour. Heat the oil in a large skillet and fry the koftas until evenly browned, turning frequently. This will take about 10 minutes.

2 Meanwhile, prepare the sauce. Heat the oil in a saucepan and fry the onion and garlic until soft but not colored. Add the remaining ingredients, except half of the olives. Bring to a boil and cook over a high heat for 10 minutes to concentrate the flavors and slightly reduce the liquid.

3 Using a slotted spoon, lower the koftas into the sauce. Cover and cook gently for about 30 minutes until the meat is cooked through and the sauce rich and pulpy. Remove about ¼ cup of the sauce and a few olives and process to a thick purée in a food processor or blender. Stir back into the sauce. Taste and adjust the seasoning, if necessary, and garnish with the parsley sprigs and remaining olives before serving.

Pineapple with hazelnuts and crème fraîche

Cooking pineapple in a grill pan works well because the high natural sugar content burns to create dramatic lines.

1 pineapple, peeled, halved lengthwise and sliced
1 cup chopped roasted hazelnuts
½ cup crème fraîche

1   Heat a grill pan or nonstick skillet until hot.

2   Place the pineapple slices on the hot surface and cook for 1–2 minutes on each side until lightly caramelized.

3   Mix the hazelnuts into the crème fraîche and serve the grilled pineapple with the nutty crème fraîche spooned over it.

Banoffi pie

It's easy when you know how—just crumble, press, and chill, then slice, toss and whip … and you've got an all-time favorite dessert.

8 oz plain graham crackers
½ cup butter

Filling:
¾ cup butter
¾ cup superfine sugar
1¾ cups condensed milk

Topping:
2 bananas
1 tablespoon lemon juice
⅔ cup whipping cream
bittersweet chocolate shavings

1   Crumble the graham crackers in a food processor or blender or place them between 2 sheets of waxed paper and crush with a rolling pin. Melt the butter in a saucepan and stir in the crumbs.

2   Press the crumb mixture evenly over the base and sides of a deep 8-inch round tart pan. Chill until firm.

3   To make the filling, place the butter and sugar in a saucepan and heat gently. When the butter has melted, stir gently. Stir in the condensed milk and bring slowly to a boil. Lower the heat and simmer for 5 minutes, stirring constantly, until the mixture becomes a caramel color. Pour the filling over the prepared crumb base and leave to cool, then chill until the mixture has set.

4   Slice the bananas and toss them in the lemon juice. Reserve one-quarter of the bananas for decoration and spread the rest over the filling. Whip the cream until thick and spread over the top. Decorate with the reserved banana slices and sprinkle with chocolate shavings.

Limeade

58

Utilize your energy in a practical way and roll the limes around quite hard on a board with your hand before you cut them open to get as much juice as you can.

6 limes
½ cup superfine sugar
3¼ cups boiling water
pinch of salt
ice cubes
mint sprigs, to decorate

1   Halve the limes and squeeze the juice into a large pitcher. Put the shells into a heatproof bowl with the sugar and boiling water. Leave to infuse for 15 minutes.

2   Add the salt, give the infusion a good stir, then strain it into the pitcher with the lime juice. Add half a dozen ice cubes, cover, and refrigerate for 2 hours or until cold.

3   To serve, place 3–4 ice cubes in each glass and pour the limeade over them. Decorate each one with a sprig of mint.

Preparation time 5 minutes + standing **Serves** 6

Grapefruit mint cooler

59

Serve this pretty cocktail in old-fashioned glasses or tumblers with crushed ice and sprigs of mint—and drink to your heart's content.

½ **cup sugar**
½ **cup water**
handful of mint
juice of 4 large lemons
1 pint unsweetened grapefruit juice
crushed ice
1 cup soda water
mint sprigs, to decorate

1 Place the sugar and water in a heavy-based saucepan and stir over a low heat until the sugar has dissolved. Leave to cool. Crush the mint leaves and stir them into the syrup. Leave to stand for about 12 hours, then strain.

2 Add the lemon and grapefruit juices to the strained syrup and stir well. Fill 6 glasses with crushed ice and pour the cocktail into the glasses. Add the soda water, then decorate each glass with a mint sprig.

Variation:
Cranberry Mint Cooler

Substitute cranberry juice for the grapefruit juice and prepare as in the main recipe.

Relaxed

Sometimes you simply have to cook a meal, but you don't want to spend hours in the kitchen when you'd far rather put your feet up and unwind. These quick and easy dishes should have you in and out of the kitchen in a matter of minutes, allowing you to spend your valuable time savoring a delicious meal on the couch or in your favorite armchair. Each of these recipes has been specially designed to leave the dinner table out of the equation, be it a one-bowl meal to be eaten with chopsticks or a dish that lends itself perfectly to being eaten with your fingers. So unwind, relax, and bon appétit!

Appetizers and snacks

Main courses

Desserts

Drinks

Toasted radicchio and fontina bruschetta with anchovy relish

It's not just easy—it's so quick that if you blink and make yourself a cocktail, you won't even remember preparing it!

1 small radicchio head

4 oz Fontina cheese

2–3 tablespoons olive oil

4 slices of rustic Italian bread, preferably one day old

1 garlic clove, peeled but left whole

2 tablespoons anchovy relish, or to taste

salt and pepper

Parmesan cheese shavings, to serve

1 Trim the radicchio, discarding any discolored leaves. Cut it lengthwise into quarters, wash, and leave to dry. Cut the Fontina into thin slices and slip them in between the leaves of the radicchio.

2 Heat half the oil in a large skillet, add the radicchio, and fry gently for 2–3 minutes, then carefully turn and cook for a further 2 minutes until the radicchio is golden and the cheese has melted.

3 Meanwhile, toast the bread on both sides and rub all over with the garlic clove, drizzle with a little oil, and spread each one with anchovy relish. Season with salt and pepper.

4 Top the bruschetta with the radicchio, scatter over the Parmesan, and serve immediately.

Braised chive flowers with shrimp

The Southeast Asians know a thing or two about flavor and it need not take ages to achieve—just 10–15 minutes.

1 tablespoon peanut oil

2 garlic cloves, crushed

6 oz flowering chives, large chives or scallions, cut into 3-inch lengths

1 tablespoon Thai fish sauce

3 tablespoons dark soy sauce

2 teaspoons superfine sugar

8 oz raw shrimp, peeled and roughly chopped

red chiles, sliced, to garnish

Thai jasmine rice, to serve (optional)

1 Heat the oil in a wok or large skillet, add the garlic, and stir-fry for 1 minute. Add the chives or scallions, fish sauce, soy sauce, and sugar, and stir-fry for 1 further minute.

2 Add the raw shrimp to the wok and stir-fry for 3 minutes until pink and cooked through. Serve immediately, garnished with red chiles. Thai jasmine rice makes a good accompaniment.

Butternut squash risotto

There's something surprisingly therapeutic about stirring a risotto, and this one tastes especially good.

66

1 butternut squash, weighing 2 lb

3 tablespoons olive oil

4½ cups chicken or vegetable stock

½ cup butter

1 garlic clove, chopped

1 onion, finely diced

1⅔ cups arborio or carnaroli rice

1¼ cups grated Parmesan cheese

salt and pepper

pumpkin seed oil, to serve (optional)

Oven temperature: 425°F

1 Preheat the oven to 425°F. Top and tail the squash, cut in half around the middle, then pare away the skin from the larger half without losing too much of the flesh. Cut in half lengthwise, remove the seeds, and cut into 2-inch dice. Repeat with the other half. Place on a large baking sheet, drizzle with 2 tablespoons of the olive oil, and season with salt and pepper. Mix well and cook at the top of the oven for 15 minutes. The squash should be soft and lightly browned.

2 Meanwhile, heat the stock in a saucepan to a gentle simmer.

3 Melt the remaining olive oil and half the butter in a heavy-based saucepan, add the garlic and onion, and sauté gently for 5 minutes; do not brown.

4 Add the rice, stir well to coat the grains with oil and butter, then add enough stock to cover the rice. Stir well and simmer gently. Continue to stir as frequently as possible throughout cooking. As the liquid is absorbed, continue adding ladlefuls of stock to just cover the rice. Continue to cook until all of the stock has been absorbed and the rice is just tender.

5 Remove the squash from the oven, add to the risotto with the Parmesan and the remaining butter, season with salt and pepper, and stir gently.

6 Serve the risotto on individual warmed plates with a little pumpkin seed oil drizzled on top of each portion, if liked.

Garbanzo bea

This unusual variation of the classic Spanish omelet is as effortless to prepare as it is delicious to eat.

6 tablespoons extra-virgin olive oil

1 onion, chopped

4 garlic cloves, crushed

½ teaspoon crushed chile flakes

1 lb chard leaves

2 cups drained canned garbanzo beans

6 eggs, beaten

2 tablespoons chopped parsley

salt and pepper

n and chard omelet

1   Heat ¼ cup of the oil in a large, heavy-based skillet. Add the onion, garlic, and chile flakes and fry gently for 10 minutes until softened and lightly golden.

2   Meanwhile, wash and dry the chard. Cut away and discard the thick central white stem. Shred the leaves. Stir the chard into the onion mixture with the garbanzo beans and cook gently for 5 minutes.

3   Beat the eggs in a bowl, add the parsley and season with salt and pepper. Stir in the garbanzo bean mixture.

4   Wipe out the skillet, then add the remaining oil. Pour in the egg and garbanzo bean mixture and cook over a low heat for 10 minutes until almost cooked through.

5   Carefully slide the omelet out onto a large plate, invert the skillet over it, and then flip it back into the skillet

6   Return the skillet to the heat and continue to cook for a further 5 minutes until cooked through. Allow to cool and serve cut into squares. Eat with your fingers.

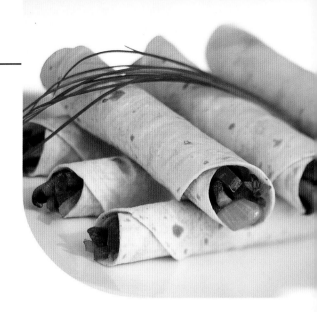

Vegetable fajitas

Quick and easy, these are just the thing to pile onto a plate and eat over a napkin on the couch.

2 tablespoons olive oil
2 large onions, thinly sliced
2 garlic cloves, crushed
2 red bell peppers, cored, seeded, and thinly sliced
2 green bell peppers, cored, seeded, and thinly sliced
4 green chiles, seeded and thinly sliced
2 teaspoons chopped oregano
1 cup sliced button mushrooms
salt and pepper

To serve:
12 warmed tortillas
chives

1 Heat the olive oil in a large skillet and gently sauté the onions and garlic for about 5 minutes until they are soft and golden brown.

2 Add the red and green peppers, chiles, and oregano, and stir well. Sauté gently for about 10 minutes, until cooked and tender.

3 Add the mushrooms and cook quickly for 1 minute more, stirring to mix the mushrooms thoroughly with the other vegetables. Season the vegetable mixture with salt and pepper to taste.

4 To serve, spoon the sizzling hot vegetable mixture into the warmed tortillas and roll up or fold over. Serve hot, with chives.

Baby vegetable stir-fry with orange and oyster sauce

Ready in a flash of the pan, it's hard to believe that something this full of flavor can be so quick to make.

2 tablespoons peanut oil
18 baby carrots
18 ears baby corn
2 cups small button mushrooms
salt and pepper
cilantro, to garnish
egg noodles, to serve

Orange and oyster sauce:
2 teaspoons cornstarch
¼ cup cold water
finely grated zest and juice of 1 large orange
2 tablespoons oyster sauce
1 tablespoon rice wine or dry sherry

1   First prepare the sauce. Blend the cornstarch in a pitcher with the cold water, then add the orange zest and juice, the oyster sauce, and rice wine or sherry. Stir well to combine.

2   Heat a wok until hot. Add the oil and heat again. Add the carrots and corn and stir-fry for 5 minutes, then add the mushrooms and stir-fry for 3–4 minutes more.

3   Pour in the sauce mixture and bring to a boil over a high heat, stirring constantly until thickened and glossy. Add salt and pepper to taste. Garnish with cilantro and serve with egg noodles.

These open sandwiches are great made with fresh tuna and served on a summer's evening as a quick supper dish with a glass of chilled white wine.

Tuna steak sandwich with spinach, ricotta, and olive filling

⅔ cup pitted olives

1 garlic clove, crushed

1 bunch of basil

1 tablespoon balsamic vinegar

3 tablespoons olive oil

4 x 6 oz tuna steaks

4 slices of granary or rye bread

½ cup ricotta cheese

4 cups baby spinach leaves

salt and pepper

lemon wedges, to serve

1 Heat a grill pan or nonstick skillet until it is very hot.

2 Place the olives, garlic, basil, vinegar, and olive oil in a food processor or blender and process. Alternatively, chop by hand and mix together.

3 Put the tuna steaks in the hot pan and cook them for 1–2 minutes on each side.

4 Toast the bread, spread each slice with ricotta, top with generous amounts of spinach, and season well. Place a tuna steak on top of each sandwich, spoon over the green sauce, and serve with lemon wedges.

In the time it takes to cook the pasta, you can assemble a delicious sauce to go with it, which will literally melt in the mouth.

Fettuccine with smoked salmon and asparagus sauce

12 oz fettuccine

2 cups asparagus tips

4 oz smoked salmon, cut into thin strips

1⅓ cups heavy cream

1 tablespoon tarragon leaves

salt and pepper

Parmesan cheese shavings, to garnish (optional)

1 Cook the fettuccine in lightly salted boiling water for 8–12 minutes, or according to package instructions, until just tender. Drain and return to the pot. Meanwhile, blanch the asparagus tips in boiling water for 5 minutes, drain under cold running water, and pat dry.

2 Toss the pasta over a low heat with the asparagus, smoked salmon, cream, tarragon, and salt and pepper to taste, until heated through.

3 Transfer to a warmed serving dish and garnish with wafer-thin shavings of Parmesan cheese, if liked.

Variation:
Smoked Salmon and Mushroom Sauce

Use 6 cups mixed sliced ceps, shiitake, and oyster mushrooms instead of the asparagus. Stir-fry in 2 tablespoons olive oil for 5–7 minutes, then add to the pasta as above.

Have everything you need prepared before you start to cook, and you'll be amazed at how quickly this dish is ready.

Chicken with vegetables, noodles, and cashew nuts

¼ cup sunflower oil

1 tablespoon light sesame seed oil

1½ lb boneless, skinless chicken breast, cut into thin strips

1 large carrot, cut into thin strips

2 large bell peppers, cored, seeded, and cut into thin strips

2 cups snow peas

18 ears baby corn

5 cups cooked medium egg noodles, drained

⅔ cup cashew nuts, toasted

2 scallions, thinly sliced

cilantro, to garnish

Sauce:

1½ tablespoons cornstarch

3 garlic cloves, finely chopped

2 teaspoons finely grated fresh ginger

3 tablespoons dark soft brown sugar

6 tablespoons tamari or soy sauce

1 teaspoon Tabasco sauce

1 pint chicken stock

1   Combine all the ingredients for the sauce in a pitcher, gradually adding the stock to make a smooth liquid.

2   Combine the sunflower and sesame oils, heat half the mixture in a wok or large skillet and stir-fry the chicken strips until cooked. This will take only about 3 minutes. Remove from the skillet. Add the remaining oil mixture and stir-fry the carrot for 1 minute, then add the peppers, snow peas, and corn, constantly tossing and frying over a high heat.

3   Stir the sauce to make sure it is well blended, then pour it into the skillet. Bring to a boil and cook for a few minutes, stirring all the time, to thicken. Add the noodles and chicken, and cook for a further few minutes to heat thoroughly.

4   Pile a generous helping in the center of each of 4 warmed bowls and sprinkle over the cashew nuts, scallions, and a little of the sauce. Garnish with cilantro and serve immediately.

Thai cooking has a lot to offer in terms of rapid and flavorful meals that you can eat in a bowl with nothing more than a pair of chopsticks.

Fried rice
with pork and mushrooms

3 tablespoons oil

¼ cup bite-sized pieces of pork

1 garlic clove, chopped

1 egg

2⅓ cups cold cooked rice

1 tomato, cut into 8 pieces

1 teaspoon palm sugar or light brown sugar

3 tablespoons Thai fish sauce

1 cup sliced oyster mushrooms

1 scallion, diagonally sliced

cilantro, to garnish

1 Heat the oil in a wok, add the pork and garlic and, stir-fry for 2–3 minutes until they begin to turn golden. Break the egg into the wok and stir it around well.

2 Add the rice and stir-fry for 2–3 minutes, then add the tomato and sugar and stir-fry for 1 minute. Add the fish sauce and stir, then add the mushrooms and stir-fry for 1 minute.

3 Finally add the scallion and mix thoroughly. Turn the rice into a bowl and serve garnished with the cilantro.

Bananas in coconut milk

This oh-so-yummy dessert is simplicity itself, and quicker to prepare than the time it takes to say "coconut milk!"

1 cup coconut milk

½ cup water

3 tablespoons palm sugar or light brown sugar

1 large or 2 small bananas, diagonally sliced

rose petals, to decorate (optional)

1   Put the coconut milk, water, and sugar into a saucepan and simmer, stirring occasionally, for about 6 minutes.

2   Add the bananas and cook for 4 minutes until heated through. Decorate with rose petals, if liked, and serve hot.

83

Chocolate mousse

Incredibly rich, amazingly quick, unbelievably naughty, and utterly delicious—sheer bliss! There's nothing like it.

84

4 eggs, separated

½ cup superfine sugar

4 oz bittersweet chocolate, broken into pieces

3 tablespoons water

1¼ cups heavy cream

To serve:

¼ cup whipping cream, whipped to firm peaks

chocolate shavings

1 Put the egg yolks and sugar into a bowl and whisk with an electric beater until thick and mousse-like.

2 Melt the chocolate with the water in a heatproof bowl set over a saucepan of simmering water. Remove from the heat and let cool slightly, then whisk into the egg mixture.

3 Whip the heavy cream until it stands in soft peaks, then carefully fold into the chocolate mixture.

4 Whisk the egg whites until stiff, carefully fold 1 tablespoon into the mousse, and then fold in the rest. Pour into 4–6 cups or small dishes and chill until set.

5 To serve, top each mousse with whipped cream, then sprinkle over the chocolate shavings.

Variation: Chocolate Orange Mousse

Follow step 1 of the main recipe, then whisk the finely grated zest of 1 orange and 1 tablespoon of Cointreau into the mousse-like mixture. Proceed as for the main recipe.

Mint tea

Serve hot or iced, and enjoy the refreshing flavor of this fragrant sweet tea—just the thing to relax you after a hard day.

86

2 teaspoons Chinese green tea
¼ cup chopped mint, preferably spearmint
1 quart water
sugar, to taste

To decorate:
4 lemon slices (optional)
4 small mint sprigs

1 Rinse a teapot with boiling water. Add the tea and mint to the pot. Bring the water to a boil and immediately pour into the teapot. Leave to stand for 5 minutes.

2 Pour the tea through a strainer into warmed heat-proof glasses or small cups. Add sugar to taste and decorate each glass or cup with a lemon slice, if liked, and a sprig of mint.

Variation: Iced Mint Tea

Add the sugar to the pot with the tea and mint. After steeping, pour the tea through a strainer over cracked ice so it cools quickly. Serve in cold glasses with ice cubes, decorated in the same way.

Iced strawberry and banana shake

87

A sure winner with children, but there's a child in all of us and many are the adults who will enjoy this.

8 oz strawberries, hulled and halved

1 small banana, sliced

1 scoop strawberry sherbet

2 scoops vanilla ice cream

½ cup milk, chilled

whipped milk, to serve (optional)

strawberry halves, to decorate

1   Put the strawberries, banana, sherbet, ice cream and milk into a food processor or blender and process until smooth. Add more ice cream for a thicker shake, or more milk for a thinner drink, if you like. Serve in tall glasses, topped with whipped cream and decorated with strawberry halves.

Id

Some days you may be perfectly happy to cook up those old standbys, things you can rely on to be quick and easy, like a simple pasta dish or a time-honored baked potato. But there are bound to be times when you want to strike out, to be adventurous and try something out of the ordinary. Perhaps you've invited someone special over to dinner and you want to impress, or maybe you are tempted by a new idea, something you've never attempted before. When the mood takes you, the old tried and tested recipes just won't do. That is the time to be a daredevil, to throw caution to the wind and to dive into this chapter. Spice up your mealtimes with this fantastic collision of flavors from all over the world.

Appetizers and snacks

Main courses

Desserts

Drinks

Pork ball and

Take a walk on the wild side
and try this unusual soup—it
packs an unexpected punch.

3 dried black fungi

2 oz rice vermicelli

2⅔ cups chicken stock

2 garlic cloves, sliced

½ cup ground pork

2 tablespoons light soy sauce

1 tablespoon Thai fish sauce

1 Soak the fungi in warm water for 30 minutes, then drain
   and slice. Soak the rice vermicelli in warm water for
   20 minutes, then drain and cut into 2-inch lengths.

2 Heat the stock and add the garlic.

3 Shape the pork into little round balls. Drop them into the
   stock and simmer for 5 minutes.

4 Add the black fungi, soy sauce, fish sauce, and rice
   vermicelli. Cook for about 2 minutes, then serve.

black fungus soup

Steamboat soup

Tiger shrimp, squid, and trout jostle for space in this fabulous seafood soup from faraway Cambodia. Serve in a steamboat or fondue pot, if possible, so the soup finishes cooking at the table.

½ cup vegetable oil

1 garlic clove, thinly sliced

1 tablespoon tamarind pulp

⅔ cup boiling water

5 cups cold water

2 tablespoons Thai fish sauce

1 teaspoon superfine sugar

1 small pineapple, peeled, cored, and cut into chunks

1¼ cups quartered tomatoes

8 scallions, finely sliced

8 oz raw tiger shrimp, peeled

3 small squid, cleaned and cut into thick rings

8 oz rainbow trout fillets, cut into pieces

To serve:

handful of cilantro

handful of sweet basil leaves

2 large chiles, diagonally sliced

1 Heat the vegetable oil in a small saucepan. When it is hot, deep-fry the garlic, a few slices at a time, until golden brown. Remove the garlic and drain on paper towels.

2 Put the tamarind pulp in a bowl with the boiling water and set aside for 20 minutes to soften. Strain the liquid (discarding the pods and tamarind stones) and place in a saucepan with the cold water, fish sauce, superfine sugar, pineapple chunks, tomatoes, and scallions. Slowly bring to a boil.

3 If you are using a steamboat or fondue pot, pour the flavored stock into the hot pot over smoking coals or a flame and add the shrimp, squid rings, and pieces of fish. Simmer gently for 6–8 minutes.

4 Serve the steamboat while the fish is cooking. Top with cilantro and basil leaves, slices of chile, and the deep-fried garlic.

Steamed wontons

Wontons, filled with shrimp, pork, and water chestnuts, are the perfect Oriental fast food—short on labor, high on flavor.

16 wonton wrappers
a little oil

Filling:

6 raw shrimp, peeled
½ cup ground pork
6 tablespoons finely chopped onion
2 garlic cloves
5 water chestnuts
1 teaspoon palm sugar or light brown sugar
1 tablespoon light soy sauce
1 egg

To serve:

soy sauce
chile sauce

1 To make the filling, blend all the ingredients in a food processor or blender.

2 Place a wonton wrapper on the side of your hand over a circle formed by your thumb and index finger. Put 1 heaping teaspoon of the filling into the center of the wrapper. As you push the filled wrapper down through the circle your fingers form, tighten the top, shaping it but leaving the top open. Repeat this process with all the wrappers.

3 Put the filled wontons onto a plate and place the plate in a steamer. Drizzle a little oil on top of the wontons, put the lid on, and steam for 30 minutes.

4 Serve the wontons hot or warm, with soy sauce and chile sauce for dipping.

Briks

Originally from North Africa, briks (pronounced "breeks") should be eaten piping hot, crisp, and golden.

about 8 oz phyllo pastry, thawed if frozen
olive oil, for brushing
sesame seeds, for sprinkling

Filling:
⅓ cup olives, pitted
3 anchovy fillets
3 sun-dried tomatoes in oil, drained and chopped
2 tablespoons chopped almonds
2 tablespoons chopped mixed cilantro and parsley
3 soft-boiled eggs, chopped
lemon juice, to taste
pepper

Oven temperature: 375°F

1 To make the filling, finely chop the olives and anchovy fillets together, then mix them with the tomatoes, almonds, herbs, eggs, and lemon juice, and season with pepper.

2 Cut the pastry into eight 4 x 10 inch strips. Work with 3–4 strips at a time, keeping the remaining pastry covered with plastic wrap or a damp dish towel to prevent it drying out.

3 Brush the strips lightly with oil and place a heaped teaspoon of the filling at the top right-hand corner of each one. Fold the corner over the filling to make a triangle. Continue folding the triangle over and over along the length of the strip of pastry. Place on a baking sheet and brush with oil. Repeat until all the filling has been used.

4 Preheat the oven to 375°F. Sprinkle the briks with sesame seeds and bake for about 20 minutes until crisp and golden. Serve hot.

Chimichangas

A classic Mexican dish, chimichangas are vegetable tortillas with more than a hint of chile.

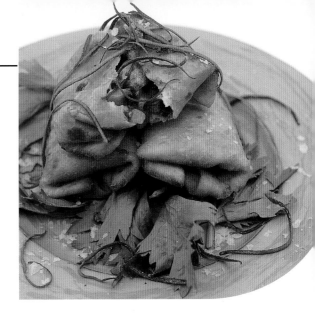

2 tablespoons olive oil

1 small onion, chopped

1 red pepper, cored, seeded, and diced

2 cups thinly sliced button mushrooms

2 tomatoes, skinned, seeded, and chopped

2 red chiles, seeded and finely chopped

1½ cups shredded Cheddar cheese

8 wheat-flour tortillas

oil, for deep-frying

sea salt and pepper

cilantro sprigs, to serve

skin of 2 zucchini, very thinly sliced into strips, to garnish

1 Heat the olive oil in a heavy-based skillet, add the onion and red pepper, and sauté until just tender but still slightly crisp. Add the mushrooms, tomatoes, and chiles, and stir-fry over a medium heat for 3–4 minutes. Season to taste with sea salt and pepper.

2 Remove the skillet from the heat and mix the Cheddar cheese into the vegetable mixture. Stir gently until the cheese melts.

3 Divide the vegetable and cheese mixture into 8 portions and put one in the center of each of the tortillas. Carefully fold the two opposite sides of the tortillas over the filling, then fold the loose edges under so that the parcel is completely sealed.

4 Heat the oil for deep-frying in a heavy-based skillet and fry the tortillas, 1–2 at a time, until crisp and golden, turning once during cooking. Remove from the oil with a slotted spoon and drain on paper towels, keeping the tortillas warm while frying the remaining batches. Serve on a bed of coriander, garnished with zucchini strips and sprinkled with salt.

Variation: Broccoli chimichangas

Make the chimichangas as in the main recipe, adding 4 cups small steamed broccoli florets to the vegetable mixture, then continue as in the main recipe. Serve with guacamole and sour cream.

Black bean kebabs with mango relish

These take a little time to make, but they're worth every last second, as we're sure you'll agree.

½ cup dried black beans

3 tablespoons olive oil

1 onion, very finely chopped

1 garlic clove, crushed

1 red chile, seeded and finely chopped

1 teaspoon ground coriander

1 tablespoon chopped cilantro

2 zucchini

24 mixed red and yellow cherry tomatoes

rice, to serve

Mango relish:

1 ripe mango, peeled and stoned

1 small onion, grated

1 red chile, seeded and finely chopped

½-inch piece of fresh ginger, peeled and grated

salt and pepper

1 Place the beans in a bowl and cover with cold water. Soak overnight, then tip into a colander and rinse well under cold running water. Transfer to a saucepan and cover with fresh water. Bring to a boil. Boil vigorously for 10 minutes, then lower the heat and simmer for about 40–50 minutes until tender. Drain well and set the beans aside.

2 To make the mango relish, place the mango flesh in a bowl and mash lightly. Add the onion, chile, and ginger and mix well. Season with a little salt and pepper and set aside.

3 Heat 2 tablespoons of the oil in saucepan. Add the onion, garlic, and chile, and cook for 5–10 minutes until the onion is soft. Add the ground coriander and cook for 1–2 minutes more. Turn the onion and spice mixture into a bowl, add the drained beans and cilantro, and mash well. Form the mixture into 24 balls.

4 Cut the zucchini lengthwise into thin ribbons and brush with the remaining oil. Thread the bean balls on metal skewers alternating with the cherry tomatoes and weaving the zucchini strips in between. Cook the kebabs under a preheated moderate broiler or on a barbecue over moderately hot coals for 4 minutes on each side. Serve with the mango relish and plain boiled rice.

Stir-fried squid with basil

This is a simple but sizzlingly-hot stir-fry, aimed at those who are sure that they can stand the heat in the kitchen.

Crispy shallots:

2½ cups peanut oil, for deep-frying

¼ cup finely chopped shallots

2 tablespoons oil

6 garlic cloves, chopped

12 small green chiles, finely sliced

1–2 shallots, chopped

4 oz squid, cleaned, cut into strips and scored in a criss-cross fashion

½ green bell pepper, cored, seeded, and chopped

2 tablespoons fish stock

1 tablespoon Thai fish sauce

1 teaspoon palm sugar or light brown sugar

½ cup basil leaves

1 First make the crispy shallots for the garnish. Heat the oil for deep-frying in a wok or deep saucepan. When it is really hot, add the shallots and stir for 1½–2 minutes until golden. Remove with a slotted spoon and drain on paper towels. When the oil is cold, it can be returned to an airtight container to use another time.

2 Heat the oil in a wok, add the garlic, chiles, and shallots and fry for 30 seconds.

3 Add the squid and green pepper, turn the heat to high, and stir-fry for 1 minute, then reduce the heat and add the stock, fish sauce, sugar, and basil. Cook, stirring, for just 1 minute more, then serve, garnished with the crispy shallots.

Crisp fried fish with chile and basil

3 garlic cloves, thinly sliced

2 cilantro roots, finely chopped

2 fresh red chiles, finely chopped

1 dried red chile, finely chopped

3 teaspoons superfine sugar

1 tablespoon oil, plus extra for deep-frying

3 tablespoons Thai fish sauce

3 tablespoons soy sauce

3 kaffir lime leaves, finely shredded

5 tablespoons fish stock or water

1 lb catfish, sea bass, or cod, filleted
   and cubed

To serve:

20–30 holy basil leaves

1 fresh red chile, shredded

A firm-fleshed white fish is deep-fried Thai-style with plenty of chile to liven things up.

1   Blend the garlic, cilantro roots, fresh and dried chiles, and sugar in a food processor or pound to a paste using a mortar and pestle.

2   Heat the tablespoon of oil in a wok or skillet and stir-fry the chile paste for 1–2 minutes. Add the fish sauce, soy sauce, and lime leaves, and stir-fry for 1 minute, then add the stock or water and bring to a fast boil. Continue boiling until the sauce has reduced a little.

3   Heat the oil for deep-frying in a saucepan. When it is hot, add the pieces of fish and fry until crisp and golden brown. Remove the fish from the oil with a slotted spoon, add to the chile sauce, and toss together.

4   Deep-fry the basil leaves for 30 seconds, remove, and drain on paper towels. Serve the fish topped with the deep-fried basil and shreds of red chile.

Sail away on an adventure of taste and discovery with this aromatic Vietnamese dish of fish wrapped in banana leaves.

Sizzling fish in banana

4 large squares of banana leaf

4 x 6 oz swordfish, snapper, or sea bass fillets, 1-inch thick

Spice paste:

1 lemon grass stalk, very finely chopped

2 large garlic cloves, finely chopped

1 kaffir lime leaf, finely shredded

2 shallots, finely chopped

½ cup butter

2 teaspoons lime juice

1 tablespoon finely chopped cilantro

1 green chile, finely chopped

1 red chile, finely chopped

salt and pepper

To serve:

boiled rice

stir-fried green vegetable

1 First make the spice paste. Blend the lemon grass, garlic, kaffir lime leaf, and shallots to a smooth paste in a food processor or with a mortar and pestle. Add the butter, lime juice, cilantro, and green and red chiles, then season to taste with salt and pepper, and blend again.

2 Put the banana leaves into a bowl, pour boiling water over them, then drain; this makes them easier to bend and wrap. Place a fish fillet in the center of each leaf and cover it with some of the spice paste. Wrap it up into a tight parcel and secure with a bamboo skewer or toothpick.

3 Chill the fish parcels in the refrigerator until you are ready to cook. Cook under a preheated hot broiler or on a barbecue for 8–10 minutes, turning once. Serve the fish still wrapped in the banana leaves. Cut open the parcels and the aromatic, buttery fish awaits. Eat with boiled rice and a stir-fried green vegetable.

leaves

Tender cubes of lamb cooked with okra and almonds are an unusual combination of flavors, surely made in heaven.

Lamb tagine with okra and almonds

2 lb boneless shoulder or leg of lamb, cut into large cubes

1 onion, chopped

3 garlic cloves, crushed

1 large red bell pepper, cored, seeded, and sliced

2-inch piece of fresh ginger, peeled and grated

2 teaspoons ground cinnamon

2 teaspoons paprika

2½ cups vegetable stock or water

1½ tablespoons clear honey

¼ cup lemon juice

12 oz okra, trimmed

⅔ cup whole blanched almonds

salt and pepper

1　Put the lamb, onion, garlic, red pepper, ginger, cinnamon, paprika, stock, honey, and lemon juice into a heavy flameproof casserole and heat just to simmering point. Cover the casserole tightly and cook for 1¼ hours, stirring occasionally.

2　Add the okra and almonds to the tagine. Cover the casserole or leave it uncovered if there is a lot of liquid left, and cook for a further 15–20 minutes until the okra is tender.

3　Season to taste with salt and pepper and serve.

Beef kebabs with beet and horseradish salsa

A hot beet and horseradish salsa is sure to make your kebabs a memorable feast.

1½ lb sirloin steak, trimmed and cut into 16 long, thin strips
8 long, woody rosemary sprigs
¼ cup balsamic vinegar
¾ cup red wine
¼ cup olive oil
1 tablespoon cracked black pepper
salt

Beet and horseradish salsa:
2 cups cooked, peeled, and chopped beets
½ red onion, finely chopped
1–2 tablespoons finely grated fresh horseradish or creamed horseradish
salt and pepper

1   Thread 2 pieces of steak onto each sprig of rosemary, concertina fashion, and place in a shallow dish. Mix the vinegar, wine, olive oil, and pepper, and pour over the steak. Turn to coat thoroughly, then cover and leave to marinate for 1–2 hours.

2   To make the salsa, mix the beets, onion, and horseradish, season with salt and pepper, and set aside.

3   Remove the kebabs from the marinade and sprinkle with a little salt. Cook under a preheated hot broiler or on a barbecue for 3–4 minutes on each side, basting frequently with the remaining marinade. Serve with the salsa.

Indian pistachio and saffron ice creams

½ cup superfine sugar

3 cardamom pods, bruised

3¾ cups evaporated milk

⅔ cup heavy cream

1½ cups finely chopped pistachio nuts

20 saffron threads, soaked overnight in
   ¼ cup hot milk

edible gold or silver leaf, to decorate (optional)

1 Put the sugar and cardamoms in a heavy-based saucepan with the evaporated milk and the cream and simmer very gently for 10 minutes. Divide the milk mixture between 2 pitchers and add pistachio nuts to one and the saffron and milk mixture to the other. Set aside to cool.

2 Pour each mixture into small kulfi or other ice-cream molds and freeze until solid. To serve, turn out onto small dessert plates and decorate with small pieces of gold or silver leaf, if using.

Flaming lamborghini

Preparation time 8 minutes **Serves** 1

A flaming cocktail mixture to set your spirit alight and enhance even the wildest of moods.

1 measure Kahlúa
1 measure Sambuca
1 measure Bailey's Irish Cream
1 measure blue Curaçao

1 Pour the Kahlúa into a warmed cocktail glass. Gently pour half a measure of Sambuca over the back of a spoon into the cocktail glass to create two layers.

2 Pour the Bailey's and blue Curaçao into two short glasses.

3 Pour the remaining Sambuca into a warmed wine glass and carefully set the Sambuca alight with a match. Pour into the cocktail glass with care.

4 Pour the Bailey's and Curaçao into the flaming cocktail glass. Drink with a straw and enjoy.

Preparation time 4 minutes Serves 1

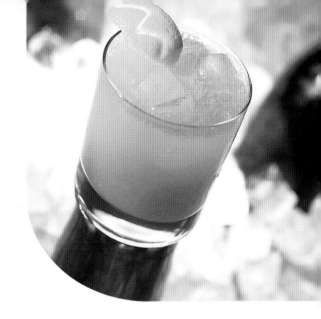

Astronaut

Mix rum and vodka with lemon and passion fruit juices, then drink slowly and head for the stars.

8–10 ice cubes
½ measure white rum
½ measure vodka
½ measure fresh lemon juice
1 dash passion fruit juice
lemon wedge, to decorate

1 Put 4–5 ice cubes into a cocktail shaker and add the rum, vodka, and lemon and passion fruit juices. Fill an Old-Fashioned glass with the remaining ice cubes. Shake the drink, then strain it into the glass. Decorate with the lemon wedge and serve.

ROMANTIC

Appetizers and snacks

Main courses

Desserts

Drinks

The link between food and romance has been made by poets and authors since time immemorial. Certain ingredients are well known for their aphrodisiac qualities, such as seafood, asparagus, and chocolate to name but three, and there are ideas in this chapter for all of them. When you are creating a romantic meal for two, you will want to spend more time enjoying each other's company than cooking alone in the kitchen, and all these recipes have been designed with this in mind. There are some more extravagant dishes that are suited to a candle-lit dinner *à deux*, while others are more suitable for sharing on the couch together during a quiet evening at home.

Mexican soup with avocado salsa

1 tablespoon sunflower oil

1 small onion, chopped

1 garlic clove, crushed

1 teaspoon ground coriander

½ teaspoon ground cumin

½ red bell pepper, cored, seeded and diced

1 red chile, seeded and sliced

1 heaping cup canned red kidney beans, drained

1⅔ cups tomato juice

1 tablespoon chile sauce

¼ cup tortilla chips, crushed

salt and pepper

cilantro sprigs, to garnish

Avocado salsa:

1 small ripe avocado

4 scallions, finely chopped

1 tablespoon lemon juice

1 tablespoon chopped cilantro

1   Heat the oil in a large, heavy-based saucepan, add the onion, garlic, spices, red pepper, and two-thirds of the chile, and fry gently for 10 minutes. Add the kidney beans, tomato juice, and chile sauce, bring to a boil, cover, and simmer gently for 30 minutes.

2   Meanwhile, make the avocado salsa. Peel, stone, and finely dice the avocado, put into a bowl and combine it with the scallions, lemon juice, and cilantro. Season with salt and pepper to taste, cover with plastic wrap, and set aside.

3   Process the soup in a food processor or blender, together with the crushed tortilla chips. Return the soup to a clean saucepan, season to taste with salt and pepper, and heat through. Serve the soup immediately with the avocado salsa, garnished with the reserved chile slices and some cilantro sprigs.

Variation: Mexican Soup with Tomato and Chile Salsa

Prepare the soup as in the main recipe and serve it with the following salsa. Put 1 cup chopped tomatoes into a bowl. Add ½ small chopped onion, 1 small crushed garlic clove, 1 seeded and finely chopped fresh chile, a pinch of sugar, and a few sprigs of cilantro. Season with salt and pepper and mix well.

Deviled oysters

Oysters have long had the reputation of being blessed with aphrodisiac qualities. Try them and see ...

12 small oysters, shucked (opened)

1 tablespoon red wine vinegar

1 teaspoon Worcestershire sauce

a few drops of Tabasco sauce

2 tablespoons butter

1 shallot, finely chopped

1 garlic clove, crushed

**⅓ cup finely chopped pancetta or
smoked bacon**

1 cup fresh white bread crumbs

**2 tablespoons freshly grated Parmesan
cheese**

1 tablespoon chopped parsley

a little olive oil

salt and pepper

1 Carefully strain the juices from the oysters into a bowl and stir in the vinegar, Worcestershire sauce, and Tabasco sauce. Cut through the muscle that attaches the oyster to the other half of the shell.

2 Melt the butter in a small saucepan and fry the shallot and garlic for 5 minutes. Add the pancetta or bacon and stir-fry for a further 3–4 minutes until browned.

3 Add the bread crumbs and pour in the oyster juice mixture. Boil until nearly all the liquid has evaporated. Remove from the heat and stir in the Parmesan and parsley, and season to taste with salt and pepper. Leave to cool.

4 Arrange the oysters in a baking dish and top each one with the bread crumb mixture. Drizzle over a little olive oil and cook under a preheated broiler for 3–4 minutes until bubbling and golden. Serve the oysters immediately.

Nigiri sushi

Light and flavorful with sensuous seafood, Japanese sushi both looks and tastes divine: perfect for a light supper on a special evening when you have other things on your mind.

123

1¼ cups Japanese short-grain rice, rinsed

1¼ cups cold water

1 tablespoon sugar

2 teaspoons salt

2 tablespoons Japanese rice vinegar

1 tablespoon wasabi paste

8 oz assorted seafood: thin slices of raw tuna, salmon or mackerel; scored and cooked squid; cooked, peeled tiger shrimp

To serve:

pickled ginger

wasabi paste

soy sauce

1   Put the rice in a heavy-based saucepan with the cold water. Cover the pot, bring to a boil and simmer for 20 minutes or until the rice is tender and the water absorbed. Remove from the heat, cover with a dish towel and leave to stand for 10 minutes.

2   Put the sugar, salt, and vinegar into a small saucepan and heat gently until the sugar has dissolved.

3   Turn the rice out of the pan into a large bowl, sprinkle with the sweetened vinegar, and toss gently with two forks to mix the vinegar dressing into the rice and to separate the grains as they cool.

4   When cool, shape walnut-sized balls of rice into ovals with wet hands. Spread a little wasabi over the top of the shaped rice and arrange a piece of fish or seafood on the top of each one. Arrange on a platter and serve with pickled ginger, extra wasabi, and soy sauce.

Spinach pancakes and asparagus gratin

1. First make the pancake batter. Sift the flour and salt into a bowl and make a well in the center. Gradually beat in the egg. Squeeze the excess liquid from the spinach. Chop the spinach very finely and beat it into the egg and flour mixture with the milk to form a smooth batter. Cover and leave to rest for 20 minutes.

2. Trim the asparagus spears and blanch in a large saucepan of lightly salted, boiling water for 2 minutes. Drain, refresh under cold water, and pat dry on paper towels.

3. Meanwhile, make the pancakes. Heat a little oil in a 7-inch skillet until it starts to smoke. Pour a ladleful of batter into the skillet and swirl to cover the base in a thin, even layer. Cook for 2–3 minutes until set, then flip with a palette knife and cook the second side for 1–2 minutes. Remove from the skillet and keep warm while cooking the remaining 3 pancakes. Brush the skillet with a little oil before adding each ladleful of batter.

4. Place 3 asparagus spears on each pancake and roll up. Place the pancakes seam side down in an oiled baking dish.

5. To make the topping, melt the butter in a small saucepan, then stir in the flour and cook over a gentle heat for 2 minutes. Gradually whisk in the milk, then slowly bring to a boil, stirring frequently, until the sauce thickens. Stir in the mustard powder and mace, and simmer very gently for 5 minutes. Season to taste with salt and pepper.

6. Pour the white sauce over the pancakes and scatter the cheese on top. Place under a preheated medium-hot broiler and cook for 8–10 minutes until bubbling and golden. Serve immediately.

Asparagus is reputed to have aphrodisiac qualities, so give it a whirl. If it doesn't work, it still tastes delicious in these pancakes.

125

12 thick asparagus spears
vegetable oil, for greasing

Pancakes:
½ cup all-purpose flour
pinch of salt
½ egg, lightly beaten
⅓ cup frozen spinach, thawed
⅔ cup milk
vegetable oil, for frying

Topping:
2 tablespoons butter
3 tablespoons flour
1¼ cups milk
½ teaspoon mustard powder
½ teaspoon ground mace
½ cup shredded Cheddar cheese
salt and pepper

Crispy wrapped shrimp

Cuddle up on the couch together and share a plate of these scrumptious shrimp—who knows what mood you'll be in afterwards?

½ cup ground pork

4 raw shrimp, peeled and minced

½ teaspoon sugar

¼ onion, finely chopped

1 garlic clove, finely chopped

2 teaspoons light soy sauce

12 raw tiger shrimp

12 egg roll wrappers

beaten egg white, for sticking

about 3¼ cups oil

basil or cilantro sprigs, to garnish

sweet and sour sauce or chile sauce, to serve

1   In a bowl, mix the ground pork, minced raw shrimp, sugar, onion, garlic, and soy sauce, then set aside.

2   Shell the other 12 shrimp, leaving the tails intact, and carefully cut open the flesh, making sure you do not cut right through the shrimp.

3   Put 1 teaspoon or more of the minced mixture onto each open shrimp. Take an egg roll wrapper and fold it almost in half, so that one corner is about three-quarters of the way towards the opposite corner. Place a shrimp on the double thickness of wrapper, leaving the tail free, and roll it up, tucking the ends in and sticking the wrapper down with a little egg white. Continue until all the shrimp are wrapped.

4   Heat the oil in a wok and deep-fry the shrimp rolls until golden—this should take about 5 minutes. Remove from the wok and drain on paper towels.

5   Garnish the shrimp with basil or cilantro sprigs and serve with a dipping sauce.

Grilled lobster tails with oregano butter

An expensive dish for a celebration, this should make your loved one feel as though you've made a special effort.

¼ cup butter, softened
large handful of oregano, chopped
2 lobster tails, halved lengthwise
salt and pepper

To serve:
1 lemon, cut into wedges
crisp salad
new potatoes

1 Put the butter and oregano in a bowl, mix, and season to taste with salt and pepper. Place the butter in a rough sausage shape on waxed paper, roll up, and twist the ends tightly, then place in the freezer to chill and harden for 10 minutes.

2 Heat a grill pan until hot. Place the lobster tails on the hot surface and cook for 5 minutes on each side. The shell will turn bright pink and the flesh white.

3 Place the lemon wedges in the hot pan for 3 minutes to warm the juice.

4 Remove the oregano butter from the freezer. Slice and arrange on top of the cooked lobsters. Serve the lobsters with the lemon wedges, accompanied by a salad and new potatoes.

A Thai-inspired recipe: Creamy coconut milk vies for attention with fiery chiles and lime. It tastes as delicious as it looks.

Coconut broiled chicken

2 boneless chicken breasts

Marinade:

1¾ cups canned coconut milk

4 garlic cloves

4 small green or red chiles

1-inch piece of fresh ginger, peeled and sliced

grated zest and juice of 1 lime

2 tablespoons palm sugar or light brown sugar

3 tablespoons light soy sauce

1 tablespoon fish sauce

¾ cup chopped cilantro leaf, stalk and root

To garnish:

1 red chile, seeded and finely diced

scallion slivers

1 To make the marinade, blend together all the ingredients.

2 Make 3 oblique cuts on each side of the chicken breasts, put them in a dish, and pour the marinade over. Cover and leave in the refrigerator for 2 hours.

3 Arrange the chicken pieces in a broiler pan, making sure they are fairly thickly spread with the marinade. Broil under a preheated hot broiler for about 15 minutes, turning occasionally. The skin side will take a little longer to cook than the other side.

4 Meanwhile, heat the remaining marinade in a small saucepan until piping hot, adding a little water if it is too thick, to make a pouring sauce.

5 When the chicken is cooked, slice it and arrange the slices on a serving dish. Serve garnished with scallion slivers and diced chile, with the sauce in a separate bowl.

Duckling flavored with peppercorns and heavy cream makes this a richly sumptuous dish.

Duckling with peppercorns

2 lb oven-ready duckling

1 tablespoon butter

2 shallots, finely chopped

5 tablespoons dry white wine

2 tablespoons brandy

1 tablespoon whole green peppercorns or
   ½ tablespoon black peppercorns, coarsely
   crushed

1 cup heavy cream

salt and pepper

chervil, to garnish

green beans, to serve (optional)

Oven temperature: 400°F

1 Preheat the oven to 400°F. Prick the skin of the duckling with a fork and season liberally with salt and pepper. Place in a roasting pan and roast for about 1¼ hours until tender.

2 Meanwhile, melt the butter in a saucepan, add the chopped shallots, and cook until transparent. Stir in the white wine and brandy, bring to a boil, and boil for 5 minutes.

3 Cut the duckling into pieces, arrange on a warmed serving dish, and keep hot. Add the peppercorns and cream to the sauce and season with salt to taste. Cook over a low heat for 3–5 minutes until thickened.

4 Spoon the sauce over the duckling and serve immediately, garnished with chervil. Green beans may be served as an accompaniment, if liked.

Broiled beef with spicy sauce

Steak in a spicy sauce is an old favorite, which will put your loved one in the mood for romance, no questions asked. Not for the faint-hearted, though.

10 oz sirloin steak

Spicy sauce:

½ **tomato, finely chopped**

¼ **red onion, finely chopped**

1 tablespoon dried ground chile

6 tablespoons fish sauce

2 tablespoons lime juice or tamarind water

2 teaspoons palm sugar or light brown sugar

1 tablespoon chicken stock or water

To garnish:

basil leaves

cilantro

flat-leaf parsley

chiles

1 Put the steak under a preheated hot broiler and cook, turning it once, according to your taste. Cook for 6 minutes for a medium-rare steak.

2 While the steak is cooking, mix together all the sauce ingredients in a bowl.

3 When the steak is ready, slice it, arrange the pieces on a warmed serving dish, and garnish with the basil, cilantro, parsley, and chiles. Serve the sauce separately.

Passion cake is so called for very good reasons: Grated carrots and walnuts combine to make a moist, mouth-watering cake with a creamy, smooth soft cheese frosting.

Passion cake

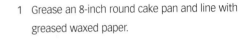

1. Grease an 8-inch round cake pan and line with greased waxed paper.

2. Melt the butter and pour into a mixing bowl. Beat in the sugar, carrots, salt, mixed spice, and eggs.

3. Sift the flour and baking powder together and add the chopped walnuts. Lightly fold into the carrot mixture until evenly mixed.

4. Preheat the oven to 350°F. Pour the mixture into the prepared pan and bake for 1 hour, until firm to the touch and golden brown.

5. Leave the cake to cool in the pan for 5 minutes, then turn out and cool completely on a wire rack.

6. To make the frosting, beat the cheese until smooth. Gradually beat in the lemon juice to taste, then beat in the sugar until well mixed.

7. Split the cake into two layers and sandwich them with one-third of the frosting. Spread the rest of the frosting over the top and sides of the cake and mark wavy lines in it with a fork. Sprinkle the top of the cake with the walnut halves.

½ cup + 2 tablespoons butter
1 cup light soft brown sugar
1 cup grated carrots
½ teaspoon salt
1 teaspoon ground mixed spice
2 eggs
1¾ cups self-rising flour
2 teaspoons baking powder
1 cup shelled walnuts, finely chopped
¼ cup shelled walnut halves, to finish

Frosting:
1 cup full-fat soft cheese
2–3 tablespoons lemon juice
½ cup confectioners' sugar, sifted

Oven temperature: 350°F

Chocolate meringue stacks

Chocolate is a time-honored arouser of passions, and served in a sauce with these meringue stacks, you should get your way every time …

138

2 egg whites
½ cup superfine sugar
1 tablespoon cocoa powder, sifted
grated chocolate and chocolate shape,
  to decorate

Bitter chocolate sauce:
6 oz bittersweet chocolate, broken into pieces
⅔ cup water
1 teaspoon instant coffee powder
¼ cup sugar

Filling:
⅔ cup heavy cream
2 tablespoons brandy
1 teaspoon clear honey

Oven temperature: 250°F

1 Whisk the egg whites until stiff, then whisk in the sugar, 1 tablespoon at a time, until the mixture holds its shape. Carefully fold in the cocoa.

2 Line 2 baking sheets with parchment paper and carefully draw eight 3-inch and eight 2-inch circles on the paper. Preheat the oven to 250°F.

3 Put the meringue into a pastry bag fitted with a ½-inch plain tip and pipe the meringue into the circles to cover them completely. Bake for 2 hours. Transfer to a wire rack to cool.

4 Meanwhile, make the bitter chocolate sauce. Place all the ingredients in a small saucepan and heat gently until the sugar has dissolved. Bring to a boil and simmer gently for 10 minutes.

5 To make the filling, whip together the cream, brandy, and honey until the mixture thickens and holds its shape, then spoon three-quarters of it onto the large meringue circles. Cover with the small circles.

6 Serve the meringue stacks on individual plates and decorate with the remaining cream. Spoon some of the bitter chocolate sauce around each one, sprinkle with a little grated chocolate, and decorate with a chocolate shape.

Champagne makes everyone feel romantic at the best of times, and blue Champagne is even more special.

Preparation time 2 minutes **Serves** 1

140

Blue champagne

4 dashes blue Curaçao

½ cup chilled Champagne or sparkling white wine

1 Swirl the Curaçao around the sides of a Champagne flute or wine glass. Pour in the Champagne and serve immediately.

Red kiss

Preparation time 3 minutes **Serves** 1

High romance: Vermouth, gin, and cherry brandy are stirred together and decorated with cocktail cherries and spirals of lemon zest. A kiss, anyone?

3 ice cubes, cracked

1 measure dry vermouth

½ measure gin

½ measure cherry brandy

To decorate:

1 cocktail cherry

spiral of lemon zest

1 Put the ice cubes into a mixing glass, add the vermouth, gin, and cherry brandy, and stir well. Strain into a chilled cocktail glass and decorate with the cherry and lemon spiral.

index